FIRST BIOGRAPHIES

Abraham Lincoln

Cassie Mayer

Heinemann Library
Chicago, Illinois

© 2008 Heinemann Library
a division of Reed Elsevier Inc.
Chicago, Illinois

Customer Service **888-454-2279**

Visit our Web site at **www.heinemannlibrary.com**

Photo research by Tracy Cummins
Designed by Kimberly R. Miracle
Maps by Mapping Specialists, Ltd
Printed and bound in China by South China Printing Company

10 09 08 07
10 9 8 7 6 5 4 3 2 1

10 Digit ISBN: 1-4034-9968-3 (hc)   1-4034-9977-2 (pb)

Library of Congress Cataloging-in-Publication Data
Mayer, Cassie.
  Abraham Lincoln / Cassie Mayer.
     p. cm. -- (First biographies)
  Includes bibliographical references and index.
  ISBN-13: 978-1-4034-9968-4 (hc)
  ISBN-13: 978-1-4034-9977-6 (pb)
  1. Lincoln, Abraham, 1809-1865--Juvenile literature. 2. Presidents--United States--Biography--Juvenile literature. I. Title.
  E457.905.M36 2008
  973.7092--dc22
  [B]
                         2007010089

Acknowledgements
The author and publisher are grateful to the following for permission to reproduce copyright material: ©Bridgeman Art Library **p. 13** (Peter Newark American Pictures); ©Corbis **pp. 6** (Bettmann), **12** (Bettmann), **16** (Royalty free), **18, 22** (Bettmann); ©Getty Images **pp. 7** (Hulton Archive), **8** (Hulton Archive), **10** (Library of Congress), **15** (MPI), **17** (MPI), **20** (Hulton Archive), **23a** (Hulton Archive), **23b** (MPI); ©The Granger Collection **p. 11**; ©Library of Congress Prints and Photographs Division **pp. 4, 5, 19, 21**; ©North Wind Picture Archives **p. 9**.

Front and back cover images reproduced with permission of the ©Library of Congress Prints and Photographs Division.

Contents

Introduction 4

Early Life 6

Slavery. .8

Speaking Out 10

A New President 12

Civil War 14

Assassination 20

Why We Remember Him. 22

Picture Glossary 23

Timeline. 23

Index 24

Introduction

Abraham Lincoln was president of the
United States. He was a great leader.

He was born in Kentucky in 1809.
He lived in a log cabin.

Early Life

When Lincoln was young, he loved to read.

When Lincoln grew up, he gave speeches about his ideas.

Slavery

When Lincoln was alive, some people were slaves.

Slaves could not choose how they lived.

Speaking Out

Lincoln spoke against slavery.

He said all people should be free.

A New President

Lincoln became president in 1861.
A president leads the country.

Many people in the South were upset.
They did not agree with Lincoln's beliefs.

Civil War

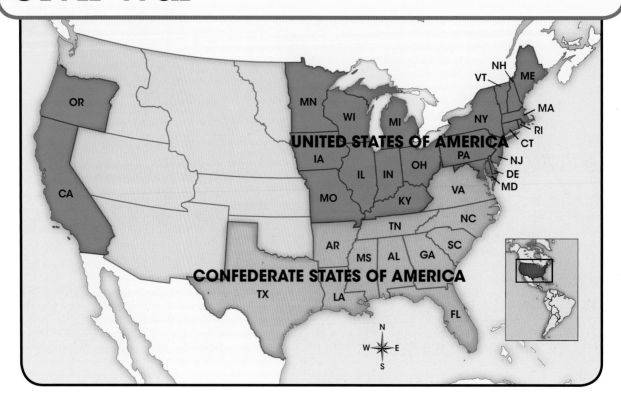

Southern states separated from the United States.

This led to the Civil War. People in the
northern states fought with people in
the southern states.

Lincoln was a good leader in war.
The war ended in 1865.

The northern states won the war.
Slaves became free.

Some people were still upset.
Some people did not agree with Lincoln.

John Wilkes Booth did not agree
with Lincoln.

Assassination

John Wilkes Booth shot Lincoln.
The shooting of a leader is called
an assassination.

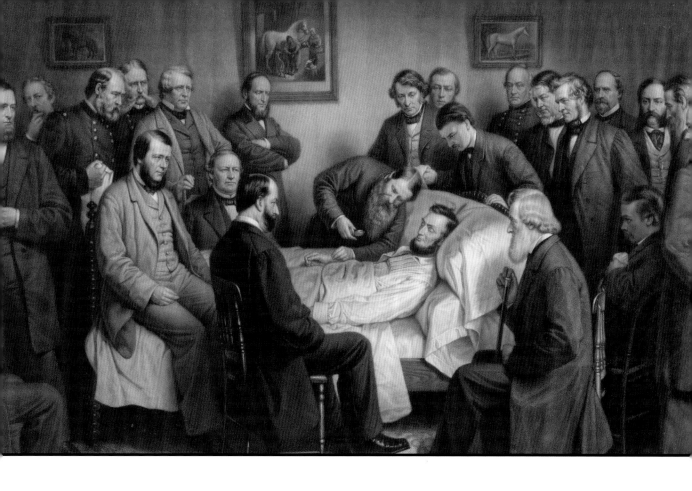

Lincoln died the next morning.

Lincoln was one of our greatest leaders.
He stood up for his beliefs.

Picture Glossary

 **assassination** the killing of a leader

 **civil war** fight between two sides in the same country

Timeline

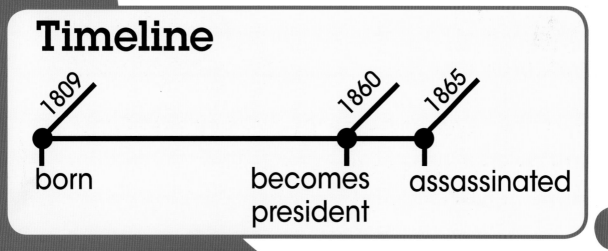

1809 — born

1860 — becomes president

1865 — assassinated

Index

Civil War, 14, 15, 16, 17

John Wilkes Booth,
 19, 20

Kentucky, 5

president, 4, 12

slave, 8, 9,
 10, 17

Note to Parents and Teachers

This series introduces prominent historical figures, focusing on the significant events of each person's life and their impact on American society. Illustrations and primary sources are used to enhance students' understanding of the text.

The text has been carefully chosen with the advice of a literacy expert to enable beginning readers success while reading independently or with moderate support. An expert in the field of early childhood social studies curriculum was consulted to provide interesting and appropriate content.

You can support children's nonfiction literacy skills by helping students use the table of contents, headings, picture glossary, and index.